What's In Your Hand?

A Believer's Guide To 3 Simple Ways To Make Money Online Using What You Already Know, Have and Do

A. Fitzgerald Hardnett

Copyright © 2024 by A. Fitzgerald Hardnett

All rights reserved. No part of this publication may be reproduced, distributed, or transmitted in any form or by any means, including photocopying, recording, or other electronic or mechanical methods, without the prior written permission of the publisher, except in the case of brief quotations embodied in critical reviews and certain other noncommercial uses permitted by copyright law.

For permission requests,and bulk orders inquiries, contact the publisher at info@consultfitz.com

"What's In Your Hands" is a self-help and business development book infused with Biblical principles for personal and professional growth. The references to Biblical teachings aim to provide guidance and insights into applying these timeless truths to everyday life and business practices.

This work is intended for informational purposes and does not intend to interpret or modify Biblical doctrine. Any interpretation or understanding of Biblical references within this book is subjective and open to individual perception.

Published by Authority Makers, a subsidiary of Social Leverage LLC.

info@consultfitz.com

ISBN: 978-1-7360160-2-2

WHAT'S IN YOUR HAND?

A BELIEVER'S GUIDE TO 3 SIMPLE WAYS TO MAKE MONEY ONLINE USING WHAT YOU ALREADY KNOW, HAVE AND DO

A. FITZGERALD HARDNETT

Table of Contents

Foreward 1
Preface 5
Unit 1: The Foundation 9
The Backstory 11
Mindset from the onset! 15
Who are you? 23
Your Chair Is In That Tree 29
Revenue Revolution 35
BeFX 43
The Digital Promise Land 49
Unit 2: The 3 Simple Ways 53
   Consulting To Cash 57
   The Power Of Mini Workshops 63
Digital Dominance 67
Absolute Clarity 75
Unit 3: Call To Action 103
Gratitude & Support 105
Arise & Shine… Your Time Has Come 114
The Offer Call™ 117
About a. Fitzgerald hardnett 122
Resources 124
Reflection Questions 125
Notes 127

FOREWARD

Proverbs 3:21 TPT wisely instructs, "My child, never drift off course from these two pivotal goals in your life: to walk in wisdom and to discover your purpose. Remember, it's these elements that truly empower you."

The Bible is a treasure trove of wisdom, offering guidance for success in every facet of life. Within its pages lie hidden gems, waiting to empower you to unearth the riches God has placed in the world. Similarly, the internet is a modern resource brimming with opportunities, ready to reveal the wealth destined for believers.

Guidance and mentorship are key to fulfilling one's purpose. Consider the example of Jesus and his disciples. Jesus, after mentoring and coaching his disciples, emphasized their need for power. This book, "What's in Your Hand," is a modern-day tool designed to awaken the entrepreneur within you. I personally love how Adrian skillfully blends spiritual principles and practical tactics that equip us for success.

"What's in Your Hand" is more than a book; it's a guide to discovering how to use your talents. It offers insights and understanding, helping you identify and nurture the entrepreneurial traits within you.

We all harbor dreams and visions of achieving greatness, of being a blessing to humanity, and leaving a lasting legacy. Often, what we lack are the knowledge and strategies to actualize our God-given talents and abilities. God's word always provides something tangible to hold onto, a foundation for our faith. This book illuminates the starting point for your journey, transforming your dreams into tangible realities.

Prepare yourself, for what you've been looking for is right here in your hands!

~Apostle Tony Brazelton

Tony & Cynthia Brazelton Ministries

Pastor Victory Christian Ministries International - Suitland Maryland

"This book is dedicated to all the Believers who know they're called to be a blessing to others but thought what they had wasn't enough…"

I gotchu…Let this book be your guide!!

What's In Your Hand?

PREFACE

The Power of Identity and Purpose

Every story has a beginning, and every journey starts with an introduction. Mine begins with a simple yet profound revelation and reminder of identity.

In the world's eye, I am many things: a husband, father, e-commerce expert, real estate investor, and more. Yet, when my son was at daycare and I had to pick him up, my accolades fell away, and I was simply "Maximilian's Dad." It's here, in that unassuming role, that the essence of my purpose was revealed.

This book is an exploration of identity—not just mine, but yours. It's about understanding the roles we play, the skills we possess, and how, when steered by purpose, they have the power to change our world and impact others. It's about recognizing that we all have a natural ability to create, which is something God put inside us right from the very start as first revealed in the opening pages of Genesis.

You hold in your hands not just a book, but your personal invitation to transform your God-given talents and ideas into streams of financial blessings for yourself and others. *What's In Your Hand* is your practical and tactical guide, offering actionable steps and insightful strategies to manifest that potential!

Within these pages lie three simple yet powerful strategies to monetize what you already know, have, and do. Grounded in biblical principles, these strategies have consistently proven their worth in the marketplace.

For some, this book will be a revelation, akin to Elisha's guidance to the widow woman in 2 Kings chapter 4, revealing untapped potential. For others, it's a reminder that the key to significant financial impact in the marketplace lies within what you already possess.

As we venture through these pages, I invite you to discover how your everyday knowledge, the skills you overlook, can become the foundation of financial freedom and impact. From the divine law of creation to the introduction of online educational enterprises, this is more than a guide—it's a journey from understanding to action, from potential to profits.

Are you ready to discover what's truly in your hand?

What's In Your Hand?

UNIT 1:
THE FOUNDATION

What's In Your Hand?

THE BACKSTORY

"Boy, do what I told you to do, and use what I gave you"
- *my momma Fredicia Hardnett*

Moses received a divine assignment from God to liberate His people from the bondage of the Egyptians. His message was clear, "Let my people go!" Yet, Moses harbored doubts and reservations, fearing that people might not believe him. He didn't think he was qualified.

In response, God posed a pivotal question.

"What is That In Your Hand?"

This question prompted a shift in Moses's perspective, steering his focus from what he lacked to what he already possessed – his staff. This moment is crucial, as it mirrors a common oversight among believers. Often, we fail to recognize our own resources and gifts, playing small even when the tools for big breakthroughs are within our grasp.

Moses, recognizing that his staff was the answer to God's question, then threw it on the ground, per God's instruction. This directive is not just about him using his gift… but about taking deliberate action.

God's call for Moses to throw the staff, and not merely drop it, underscores the need for the intentional application of our gifts.

This act of intentionality is what we, too, must do in order to liberate others from their personal 'Egypts.'

However, once he executed God's command, Moses initially reacted with fear and retreated. This reaction is not uncommon. Many of us identify a gift or talent within ourselves but are too frightened to embrace it, instead of applying it purposefully, we abandon it and flee.

But check this out… just as God instructed Moses to reclaim his staff, I invite you, through this book, to do the same with your gifts.

You are called to aid in the liberation of others, and your talents and gifts are reminders of your purpose and God's plan for you. It's time to acknowledge, embrace, and actively utilize your gifts. Romans 8:19 says, "The Earth itself is in anguish, groaning, awaiting the manifestation of God's children."

The world is waiting for you to stop running from what's in your hand and do

what God told you to do with it.

Arise and shine! You are the beacon of light for society's darkness!

What's In Your Hand?

MINDSET FROM THE ONSET!

"What you think about, you bring about! You are the lump sum of your most dominant thoughts."
-A.Fitzgerald Hardnett

Why talk about mindset first?

We must address your mindset right away because if we don't, nothing I teach you later will make a difference. It will be worth-less if we pour this information into an old mindset.

The Bible says you can't pour new wine into old skins, so I'm here to change the way you think so that I can increase your capacity for new things.

By the time you finish this book, you will believe that you can make money online using what you already know, have, and do. Plus you will have the EXACT blueprint to make it happen!

What do you believe?

I've discovered that to make money online there are a few simple things that you must believe, I call them the…

Believer's Business Building Blocks

1. We can do more good for the Kingdom with money than without it [Genesis 12:2-3]
2. You must solve a problem that the marketplace considers valuable [2 Kings 4:7]
3. You must believe that you have at least 1 gift that can make you wealthy [Matthew 25: 14-30]
4. You must believe that you are worthy of the four or five-figure investment that your clients will make to work with you [Luke 10:7]
5. You must believe that there are people out there looking for you, and your solution who have the money and are happy to pay you to help them [Matthew 9:37]
6. You embrace selling and are okay with doing it often [Proverbs 11:26]

7. Money isn't bad, being greedy is [Ecclesiastes 10:19]
8. You must plant seeds, allow time for cultivation, and then put in the work, to reap the harvest [Genesis 8:22]
9. Faith is necessary to make all of this work [James 2:18]

That's it!!

If you are not fully persuaded on any of these business building blocks, then you will sabotage your success, and cap your earning potential.

Here is why these are important:

During your journey, you will have a multitude of thoughts and I would dare say that 95% of your thoughts as an entrepreneur can be categorized into one of two thought patterns.

Your thoughts are either income-*producing* or income-*reducing*!

When you think a thought like ' I can't do that (whatever that is) because of (insert whatever excuse you'd like here)', then this thought immediately becomes income REDUCING. It is limiting what you believe is possible, and the Bible clearly says that as a man thinks in his heart, so is he (Proverbs 23:7).

To create income PRODUCING thoughts you must focus on what is possible. Focus on what you have, what you *can* do, and who God says you are. Followed closely with the reassurance that all things are possible to those who believe (Mark 9:23).

This is why we <u>*MUST*</u> address your mindset right away.

What you think about… you bring about!

Thinking and Speaking: The Power of Mindset

Since we're focusing on mindset from the onset, let me break thinking and speaking down for you.

Words are containers or seeds. They carry whatever is in your thought life. What the seeds (words) contain could be the power of life & death, blessing or cursing... it's totally up to you.

One of the first things that you, as a Believer, must do to really shift your world is to <u>*RENEW YOUR*</u>

MIND and change your words. This hint comes from Romans 12:2.

You must switch up, and exchange your current vocabulary for Faith-filled words that move mountains... not words that empower mountains to remain in your life.

God gives us a choice in Deuteronomy 30:19 to choose between life and death, blessings and curses, then He gives us a hint... choose life.

The next logical question is...

So, how do I choose life Fitz?

Say this aloud:

> *"I must guard my heart with all diligence because my life is shaped by my thoughts and words."*

Now let that thought sink in a bit...

What gets down inside your heart, or thoughts, comes out of your mouth and your life.

1. Death and life are in the words that you speak. This is why Proverbs 18:21 says that we will eat the fruit of our mouths because words are seeds and they will produce a harvest.
2. The Bible makes it clear that our hearts and minds are like a thermostat in a house, controlling the environment of our lives. That's why monitoring and protecting our thoughts is so important.
3. But let's be real, this isn't the easiest task. Every day in life we see and hear stuff that is counterproductive to our success (think tv and music).

Here is a visual roadmap of how to choose life through our mindset.

How To Choose Life!
2.
Matthew 12:34
... what fills the heart comes out the mouth
-Common English Translation

1.
Proverbs 4:23
Guard your heart more than anything else, because the source of your life flows from it.
-Gods Word Translation

3.
Proverbs 18:21
Death and life are in the power of the tongue, And those who love it and indulge it will eat its fruit and bear the consequences of their words.
-Amplified Translation

Faith is created in the ears because faith comes by hearing and hearing by the Word of God.

Doubt is created in the eyes, this is why the Bible tells us not to be moved by what we see.

We need to protect our hearts because what we think/how we think, shapes our lives.

What gets into your heart comes out of your mouth. The words that come out of your mouth are either weapons of mass destruction or seeds of mass production… simple as that.

Fitz Fact™

"Your Mindset begins with what you hear"

Put God's words of healing, prosperity, and peace before your eyes, in your ears, and in your heart. Then speak them out in faith, and bring your heart and tongue in line with the WORD of God.

Stop reporting the facts, and start believing and speaking the promises of God for your life and business.

Go to

www.WhatsInYourHand.xyz/resources

For 15 Word-based affirmations that you should use daily.

WHO ARE YOU?

"Earn, learn, fear, hear, heart – at the root of all these is 'ear.' We become the product of what we hear."

- A. Fitzgerald Hardnett

Imagine meeting someone new. You introduce yourself by highlighting what defines you in that context. Similarly, when someone else introduces you, they pinpoint what's crucial about you in that scenario.

For example, I am a husband, father, brother, son, and uncle. I am also an e-commerce expert who has generated over six figures in a month, $27,000 in one day and $5,000 in 50 minutes all through e-commerce, specifically, selling t-shirts online. As well as a real estate investor who has made over $240,000 in profit in a single deal. Yet, none of that stuff matters when my son introduces me to one of his buddies. The first thing he tells people is… Hey, this is my *Dad*!

Let's stay there for a moment.

Back in the day when I would go to pick my son up from daycare, the first thing they asked me to confirm and verify was my identity before I was allowed into the building.

They weren't interested in my business acumen or my other accomplishments and titles. What mattered to them was who I was and whether I belonged there. They sought confirmation of a connection relevant to their context – a measure taken to ensure the safety of my son and the other children. My admission into the building was granted solely because I identified myself as Maximilian's Dad. At that moment, that was the most crucial piece of information they needed to know about me.

Just as my identity as Maximilian's dad was most important in the daycare setting, the first introduction we get of God in Genesis highlights what's mandatory for us to know about Him.

God does the same exact thing. The first thing we are told about God, is that He created the heavens and the Earth.

Why is that the first thing we're told?

Because the most important thing that God wanted us to know about Himself is that He is Creative.

In Genesis 1:2, it says the Earth was formless and empty, darkness was over the surface of the deep and the Spirit of God was hovering over the waters.

So when I read those first two verses I'm introduced to a God who lets us know that He's creative and then right behind that, He identifies a problem.

The problem was a world described as being 'formless, empty, and dark'. Then in verse three, He solves the problem by creating a solution with His words, "and God said let there be light and there was light…" Problem solved!

The next nugget is found in Genesis 1:26, God is having a conversation with the Holy Spirit, and He has an idea to create man in Their image to dominate, so what does He do?

He creates man in His image.

But what was God's image you ask?

Fitz Fact™

We are made in the image of "a creative, problem solver, who uses His words to create the world that He wants to see."

And with that image, God gives us the EXACT SAME power to execute, when He gave us what I call the First Command, and it was simply to be fruitful, multiply, replenish, and subdue the whole Earth. - Genesis 1:28

The next thing that I want to bring to your attention is in Genesis chapter 2 verse 4; It says God had finished the work HE had been doing…

This is important to highlight because now we know that working to create the world that you want to see is an honorable thing. *After all, it's a God thing!*

This discredits the lottery or jackpot-chasing mentality and also disrupts believers waiting and praying for money and houses to fall from the sky and calling it 'waiting on God'. This shows us that our results are in direct correlation to our work and it is normal to work for what we want.

Further in Genesis chapter 2, verses 4-15, we see a world awaiting cultivation, which is a problem requiring a solution.

God's response?

He breathes life into man and places him in the Garden of Eden to work it and take care of it.

Why did I take you through that journey?

Because too many believers move and think as if they are helpless and have no power to change their situation. That's simply not the case!

Our Godly heritage shows us that you and I are creative problem solvers, that shape the world that we want to see with our words and our work!

You have the power to change your world!

So, within these pages, I am going to illuminate and reveal more hidden truths and lay a trail that helps connect the dots. I'll give you three simple ways for you to generate money online using what you already know, have, and do.

Now that you know who you are, are you ready to get to work?

YOUR CHAIR IS IN THAT TREE

"The world we desire isn't granted; it's built. Every dream demands the alignment of our will and our words multiplied by the sweat of our brows"
- A.Fitzgerald Hardnett

Have you ever wanted something so bad, but never got it? As a child, I knew that feeling all too well. Despite their best efforts, my parents often couldn't provide what I wanted. I'm the oldest of four children who grew up with two hard-working parents in the '70s, so there's that! Once, I asked my father for a BMX bike (probably more than once, but you know what I mean). Do you know what this joker did?

He walked me outside to the shed and presented me with a lawnmower, saying, "Son, everything you want can be found on the other side of this lawnmower. You want a bike, it's on the other side of this lawnmower."

Confused and frustrated, I'm thinking, "What in the world?" Pop, I asked for a bike, not a lawnmower!

To make it so bad, I had never even cut grass before. What was he thinking?

I was pissed, to say the least!

How was an old, raggedy lawnmower going to lead me to my bike?

Well, he showed me how… despite my doubts.

I started my first 'business', cutting grass. Those $10 jobs might not have seemed like much, but they taught me a crucial lesson, and I share that lesson below.

Although I didn't understand my father's words then, I never forgot them. His words didn't fully resonate with me until years later when I came across a book *Faith & The Marketplace* by Bill Winston. This book unlocked a profound and pivotal concept: *"The things that believers want like cars, houses, money, or any other blessings don't just fall from the sky. That's not how God operates."*

God gives us what I call the VIP Treatment, **V**isions, **I**deas, & **P**urpose mostly in seed form, and we have to cultivate them into our desired reality.

The fact is, it's going to take time for some of this stuff to develop and grow to a point where it provides for you and others continuously. That's why, in James 1:4 the Bible tells us that we are in need of patience so that we may be perfect and entire, lacking in nothing.

Consider a chair: once a mere tree.

I imagine way back in the day someone viewed sitting on the ground as a problem that needed to be solved. Then they had a vision, which was in seed form. In order for them to turn that vision into reality, they had to go to work and put in the required effort to create what they envisioned.

Work isn't just necessary; It's how we realize our God-given gifts.

Now, let's tie this into a Biblical principle to give you a foundation to stand upon.

The Biblical principle in James 2:17 echoes this: "faith by itself, if it does not have works, is dead."

My father's advice, paired with Winston's insight, showed me the way.

The money I wanted would come from those I served—through work.

And here lies the principle I discovered:

Fitz Fact™

"All the money you want to make is in the hands of those you are here to help. It is accessed through the valuable solutions you offer, through work!"

In Genesis 2:2 we're told about the completion of the heavens and the Earth.

2 "And on the seventh day God ended his **WORK** which he had made; and he rested on the seventh day from all his **WORK** which he had made.

3 And God blessed the seventh day, and sanctified it: because that in it he had rested from all his **WORK** which God created and made - Genesis 2:2-3 KJV

Notice how I have emphasized the word "work" ; it is repeated three times in just two short verses.

That's no coincidence.

If God had to work to create the world which He wanted to see, so must we!

It's clear that work is a good thing, because work is a God thing!

This is a Kingdom Principle. We too, must embrace work to create the world that *we* want to see.

Say this aloud:

"I embrace work. Work is a good thing because work is a God thing!"

Perhaps you're facing financial challenges, or you're not making the money you desire, consider this...

"The money you wish to make is tied to your unique purpose, your divine assignment, and all it takes is for you to go to WORK!!

Just as the chair started as a tree, your desired earnings are waiting to be unlocked through your efforts.

Yes, you have to go to work.

Not just any work, but your calling!

The work that serves others by walking in your purpose

Let this truth transform your life. Let it inform your efforts, for through work, what you desire can and will become attainable.

Are you ready and willing to work to create the world you desire to see?

Kingdom Success Principle

Your God-given power to get wealth will appear in seed form first, small and insignificant. You must acknowledge it, cultivate, and develop it into its ultimate income-producing state.

REVENUE REVOLUTION

"If you need money, go to the marketplace with a solution to a problem that motivated people want solved"

- A.Fitzgerald Hardnett

Stop begging and waiting for a blessing to 'fall from Heaven', that's not how any of this works.

Let's look at a powerful story of how a woman in 2 Kings 4 used what was in her hand to change the financial destiny of her family.

My interpretation and viewpoint of the verses will be [inside these brackets after the verses].

2 Kings 4:1 "Now the wife of a son of the prophets cried to Elisha your servant my husband is dead, and you know that you're servant feared the lord but the Creditor has come to take my two sons to be a slaves

[This lady has recently become a widow, and her husband left them in a pile of debt, so the creditors are coming to take away her sons as collateral. Her motivation level on a scale of 1-10, with 10 being absolutely ready to do whatever is necessary, she was about a 13! So, she goes to the man of God Elisha for help and she feels a bit entitled to his help because her husband served them.]

V2: Elisha said to her what should I do for you tell me what have you of sell value in the house, she said your handmade has nothing in the house except a jar of oil

[Elisha is like 'ok, what do you want me to do about it? Matter of fact, tell me what you have in your house that you can make money with?'

Her reply to the question is, "I don't have anything... well, nothing, except a little oil."

She answers his question from a position of desperation, one of having an entitled victim's mindset. Perhaps it is the pressure of the situation or the fact that she has not had to work her TAGS

(Talents, Abilities, Gifts & Skills) in quite some time, and they have been buried under years of non-use.

... and then it hits her. I have a little oil.

Which sounds like people who say things like 'I do have this one thing, but I haven't used it in a very long time, and honestly up until now, I had forgotten all about it because I don't know how to really monetize it.'

Does this sound familiar?

So many of us have been given talents and gifts, but we have failed to move on them because we've minimized them.

This happens because those gifts come super easy to us. Somewhere along our journey, we've accepted the thought that if it comes easy to us, that it's not worth anything, so we end up devaluing it and/or giving it away for free.

Elisha asked her a powerful question, because questions steer focus, He got her to go from being a victim to being resourceful, all with a simple question.

This is important because her solution (your solution) is going to **_come out of you, not outside of you._**

He forces her to focus on what she DOES have and not focus on what she does not have.

He awakened her to new possibilities because while she had the victim mentality she was closed to any other options which is why she said 'I have nothing' at first, then added 'well except this jar of oil.'

Her response is like so many of you who are reading this book. You have something of value, you just don't know how to use it in the marketplace to make money… this book is going to empower you to change that!]

Authors Invitation

If this challenge resonates with you, then I invite you to schedule a discovery call so that we can help you through this faster…

www.WhatsInYourHand.com/call

V3 Then he said go around and borrow vessels from all your neighbors empty vessels and borrow

not a few

[He gives her the instructions and adds what I call a peculiar ending, 'borrow not a few'. This last statement gives us some insight into just how wise this Prophet, Elisha, really is. He tells her not to stop at reasonable efforts. What you think is enough, won't be, go beyond your comfort zone.

As you read this book, you will need to take action that is absolutely beyond your comfort zone because what may seem reasonable, will not be enough to get the results that you desire.]

V4 And when you come in shut the door upon you and your sons then pour out the oil you have into all those vessels, set it aside each one when it's full

[He gives her the actual plan and tells her to separate from people, assemble her team, and then execute. I like this verse because it introduces processes, systems, and legacy. This allows her sons to be a part of the faith process, and the separation keeps her faith from being contaminated by her neighbors.]

V5 So she went from him and shut the door up on herself and her sons who brought to her the vessels as she poured the oil

[This is her beginning to apply her faith and execute the plan by creating a system of duplication & multiplication. I picture that her process went something like this:

Step 1 - The younger son brought her the empty jars

Step 2 - She would pour the oil into it

Step 3 - The older son would grab it and set them aside once they were full

Step 4 - Repeat

Question: What is your process for production?]

V6 When the vessels were all full she said to her son to bring me another vessel and he said to her there is not a one left. Then the oil stopped multiplying

[This verse is another powerful point that gets missed. The woman never expected the oil to stop flowing, why do I say that? Because she asked for another jar, but there wasn't one available, so the oil stopped multiplying.

Here is the lesson that most entrepreneurs miss, don't try and fill a jar when there isn't any demand for your oil!

Kingdom Success Principle

"Don't try and create solutions to problems that the marketplace is not demanding, or willing to pay for."

I can imagine the look of confusion on her face… she is like, ummm ok what now???]

V7 Then she came and told the man of God. He said, Go sell the oil and pay your debt and you And your sons live on the rest.

[So she goes back to Elisha, the man of God, and tells him something like 'I got a whole house filled with jars of oil, and I'm still broke and in debt!' He probably chuckles at her dilemma.

He instructs her to go sell the oil and pay your debts and you and your sons live on the rest…

Now here is what he DIDN'T tell her to do…go give it all away. He didn't tell her that God will provide or to keep praying, fasting, and believing either. No, he told her to take that oil down to the marketplace and *do business, by selling the oil.*

She was providing solutions to problems that people have and want solved. Remember, her neighbors' jars were empty when she gathered them. She was their solution.]

BeFX

"Every product is a brick in the wealth-building journey, laying the foundation for financial growth and prosperity"-A.Fitzgerald Hardnett

In this chapter, we'll explore another crucial Biblical principle, one that major corporations have used to consistently establish their market dominance. Unfortunately, the Body of Christ has often overlooked this principle.

If I were to ask you to identify the industry and makers of certain products, you'd likely find it quite easy...

Think about how readily you can associate these common products with their manufacturers and the industries they belong to: Whopper™, Big Mac™, Accord™, F-150™, or iPad™

This recognition isn't accidental but rather the outcome of consistently applying the Law of Domination.

Now, let's dissect this principle and demonstrate its straightforward implementation.

I've named this principle **"The Law of Domination"** or "The 1st Command," deriving its essence from Genesis 1:28:

"And God blessed them, and God said unto them, Be fruitful, and multiply, and replenish the earth, and subdue it: and have dominion."

To establish dominion, one must engage in production - a simple yet profound truth.

Consider the layout of your local grocery store. As you walk in, you're often greeted by fruits and vegetables in the 'produce section.'

But why do we call it the produce section?

Because it's where you'll find the fruits of someone's labor - seeds planted, nurtured, and harvested, now ready for purchase and consumption. Foods that farmers have *produced*.

In the marketplace, just as in the grocery store's produce aisle, the act of producing, combined with selling, plays a crucial role in business growth and expansion.

If you aspire to build wealth, your initial step must involve production.

Follow along as I dissect this principle and demonstrate its straightforward implementation.

Be Fruitful:

Begin by creating a valuable solution to a big problem.

Multiply:

Ensure that your initial solution can be easily replicated.

Replenish:

Establish a system that distributes or refills your offering without your direct daily involvement.

Subdue:

Give your product a distinctive name, making it the go-to source while avoiding market confusion.

Now, let's examine a real-world example of this law in action, as demonstrated by Apple Inc.

Remember, businesses exist to solve problems profitably.

Consider Apple's release of the iPod. What problems did it solve?

- Bulky music storage
- Limited space
- Slow file transfer
- Short battery life and other issues

Apple didn't merely create an innovative product; they embodied the Law of Domination:

First, they invented the iPod, addressing a widespread problem that many people sought a solution for - *#BeFruitful*

Next, they didn't stop at just one unit; they established a system for mass production, replicating their solution by the thousands - *#Multiply*.

The third step involved creating a replenishment system or distribution process, utilizing partnerships and retail stores. This eliminated the need for Steve Jobs or Tim Cook to hand-deliver each product - *#Replenish*

The final crucial step was giving this device a unique name. It wasn't just another MP3 player; it was uniquely branded as the 'iPod,' solidifying its market position and separating it from the competition - *#Subdue*

This is the Law of Domination in action, operating invisibly in our daily lives.

What's In Your Hand?

THE DIGITAL PROMISE LAND

"In order to dominate you must produce a solution, build it once then sell it twice" - *A.Fitzgerald Hardnett*

What is open 24 hours a day, 7 days a week, 365 days a year; it never sleeps nor slumbers?

The internet

God gave a glimpse of this powerful tool, when he had Isaiah prophesy centuries ago about our gates being open continually, day and night, so that people can bring us the wealth of nations. (Isaiah 60:11)

 This passage perfectly describes the internet - a digital gateway that's never closed, not even when big government closed everything else around us, like during the 2020 lockdowns. The internet remained open, 24/7, a never-sleeping marketplace, a

Digital Promise Land where dreams are not just sown, but also harvested.

Believers, this is our moment to leverage what's in our hands and combine it with the power of the internet. The internet is a gift, a tool to help us rise and shine, to showcase our light. It's the platform where promises of wealth transfer are not just dreams but can be realized practically, as nations come to our shining light.

It's our opportunity to go out into all the world and preach the good news that the problems people are suffering with can be solved easily. The Bible says that the harvest is plentiful, but the laborers are few. I take this to mean that the opportunity to use the internet as a digital harvesting machine is wide open, but few believers are leveraging this technology to their full advantage.

The internet provides a Digital Promise Land, where the seeds of your ideas can grow into towering trees of success, watered by the rivers of global connectivity and nurtured by the sunlight of innovation.

So, I challenge you to embrace the internet for all it offers. It's our world stage and our open gate, leaning into this tool and learning how to leverage it is a must.

What's In Your Hand?

UNIT 2:
THE 3 SIMPLE WAYS

What's In Your Hand?

MENTAL MONEY

"True wealth doesn't lie in the labor of your hands, rather it's encompassed in the knowledge within your head. It is your intellect that can be packaged and passed down profitably for generations."- A.Fitzgerald Hardnett

If you were to ask me what type of business to start, so that you can begin to use these principles to your advantage. Here is what I'd say...

1. Become a consultant
2. Host Paid workshops
3. Create a digital product business

Those are the three simple ways to use what you know, have, and do to make money online.

What I absolutely know to be true is this:

Fitz Fact™

"There is infinitely more money in what you know than what you can do with your two hands."

What's In Your Hand?

CONSULTING TO CASH

The fastest way that I know to make money online using what you already know, have and do is to become a consultant. A consultant provides expert advice professionally. You can answer questions for people, tell them what to do, how to do it, and get paid for it!

Fitz Fact™

"When you consult, your knowledge is the product being sold!"

King Solomon was a consultant, and the Bible tells us in 1 Kings 10:24 that annually people came from all over the world to hear Solomons' wisdom and they brought gifts!

Why Consulting?

1. Immediate Monetization of Skills: If you have expertise in a particular area, consulting allows you to monetize it quickly. You don't need to create a product or develop a complex business model; your knowledge is the product.

2. Freedom and Flexibility: Consulting can often be done remotely, this means you don't have to fight traffic or go into any office, unless you choose to. This grants you the flexibility to work from anywhere. This freedom is very attractive and a significant advantage in today's ever evolving digital world.

3. High Demand: Almost every industry has a demand for expert consultants. Whether it's marketing, finance, health & wellness, technology, or even niche areas like gardening or dog obedience. There is always someone looking for expert guidance.

4. Easy To Get Started: The minimum that you need to start with is

- Expertise in a high demand field
- Online scheduling software
- Video conference platform that has recording capabilities
- Document sharing and collaboration tools

- Merchant account or online payment processor
- Email service provider

Go here for an up to date list of tool recommendations
www.WhatsInYourHand.xyz/resources

You can consult people on ANYTHING that you know how to do, as long as you can get the attention of the audience that needs that transformational information.

What are you good at? What do you enjoy doing? Your consulting niche should align with your skills and passions. Remember, the more specialized your expertise, the more valuable it is.

Did you know that the moment someone asks you for help or guidance to solve their problem, you're a consultant (albeit often unpaid) but still a consultant? <u>People already see you as an expert in something.</u> The problem is you don't see yourself as an expert... YET. You have most likely been giving away your expertise, or intellectual property, for free for far too long.

This is way too common, especially if it's something that comes easy to you. We've been conditioned to think that if it comes easy to us, then it isn't valuable to the marketplace. We say stuff like, 'Nobody's gonna pay me to do that,' so you don't value it enough to put a price on it. However, it's super valuable and other experts are getting paid for the exact same thing.

Listen to me, friend, and hear me good…

"STOP GIVING AWAY FOR FREE, WHAT GOD GAVE YOU TO BRING IN A FEE!"

-A.Fitzgerald Hardnett

You have the ability to get paid to solve someone's problems by simply talking to them and answering their questions or giving them guidance - that's consulting.

People, AND organizations, will pay you to help them get a result faster than they could do on their own.

The key to successful consulting is simple: meet qualified people, tell them you are a consultant, offer to help them and then deliver tangible results. It is really that simple. When you help your clients achieve their goals faster or more effectively than they could on their own. This builds your reputation and leads to more business.

Some of you are corporately trained on various topics and subjects. Well guess what…if that job is paying you to do something, that means that *they* have gone out into the big marketplace and found a buyer for that service.

NEWSFLASH… all they have done is just marked up *your* labor, and you can do the exact same thing for yourself.

Consulting is a powerful way to turn your knowledge and skills into a profitable online business. It offers flexibility, a wide range of opportunities, and the potential for significant financial rewards. By focusing on delivering value and building your reputation, you can establish a successful consulting practice that not only earns you income but also contributes positively to others' success. You can have people coming from all over the world to work with you, just like King Solomon.

In the next few chapters, I am going into full detail on how you can implement this in your life.

In the next few chapters, I'll detail how you can implement this in your life.

Visit www.WhatsInYourHand.xyz/resources

For tool recommendations from the Getting Started section.

THE POWER OF MINI-WORKSHOPS

The next method I'm particularly fond of is hosting paid virtual workshops, which I like to call 'mini money magnets.'

Mini workshops are short, focused online sessions where you share your expertise on a specific topic and get participants a quick win. They stand out for their ability to swiftly generate revenue, build a dedicated email list of genuine buyers, establish your credibility, and eventually evolve into a semi-passive digital product business.

Let's explore the benefits of mini-workshops in detail. They allow you to effectively:

Build an Email List of Buyers, Not Just Freebie Seekers

The first significant advantage of mini-workshops is the cultivation of an email list brimming with actual buyers. Unlike free content that can attract 'freebie seekers' who aren't willing to invest in their solution, a paid workshop filters in those who value your knowledge enough to pay for it. This list is gold – it's filled with individuals already positioned to spend more money with you in the future. They have already demonstrated their willingness to invest in what you offer.

Establish Trust and Demonstrate Expertise

Trust and credibility are the currencies of the online world. Mini workshops allow you to showcase your expertise in real time, answering questions, and solving problems on the spot. This interaction is not just a display of knowledge; it's a demonstration of your expertise and the ability to apply that knowledge effectively. Participants leave not just educated but impressed, laying a foundation of trust that is hard to shake.

I have a created a blueprint on How to create a Quick Win Workshop For Less Than $50 bucks and then turn it into a digital product, if you'd like a copy head over to

[www.WhatsInYourHand.xyz/resources]

Low Overhead Costs, High Revenue Potential

One of the most compelling aspects of mini workshops is their cost-effectiveness. With minimal overhead – no physical venue, no travel costs, just your time and a stable internet connection – they offer a high return on investment. The revenue generation is not just theoretical; it's immediate. As soon as your workshop is live and tickets are on sale, you start earning.

From Active Engagement to Semi-Passive Income

The journey from conducting live workshops to creating a semi-passive digital product business is a natural progression.

Step 1: Record your workshop

Step 2: Refine the workshop based on feedback

Step 3: Re-package the workshop as an on-demand course or resource.

This transition allows you to continue earning from your expertise long after the live session has ended, with minimal ongoing effort.

Let's Review…

Mini workshops are more than just an online money-making method; they are a strategic tool that leverages your existing knowledge into a profitable, trust-building, and scalable online business.

With low overhead costs and the potential for quick revenue generation, they offer a practical and effective way to start your journey in the digital marketplace. As you embark on this path, remember this:

Fitz Fact™

Your knowledge is valuable, and paid, mini-workshops are your stage to showcase it.

DIGITAL DOMINANCE

The Power of Digital Products

The third way I recommend for turning what you already know, have and do into online income is creating a digital education company. This chapter dives into the transformative power of creating and selling digital products like courses and trainings.

Why Create A Digital Product Business?

Unlike traditional service-based or physical product businesses, a digital education company offers unmatched benefits such as time, location, and financial freedom, all because of its limitless potential.

The Challenges of Service Based Businesses

Service-based businesses, where your physical presence and direct labor are required, face inherent limitations such as:

- Time Constraints: With only 24 hours in a day, the amount of service you can provide is capped.
- Location Boundaries: Your ability to offer services is often limited to how far you can travel within a given time frame *AND* still be *profitable.*
- Labor Dependencies: The scale of service is directly tied to the number of staff available to perform these services.

The Challenges of Physical Product Businesses

Physical product businesses also encounter significant hurdles and challenges such as…

- Production Caps: There's a limit to how much product can be produced, often constrained by resources and manufacturing capacity.

- Shipping and Handling Issues: Logistics, like shipping disruptions experienced during events like the COVID-19 pandemic, can severely impact customer service and satisfaction.
- Staffing Limitations: Similar to service-based businesses, physical product businesses are often limited by the number of staff available.

The Limitless Potential of a Digital Product Company

In contrast, a digital education company transcends these traditional barriers and provides these benefits…

- Time Freedom: Digital products, once created, can be sold around the clock, 24/7. This creates a continuous income stream, independent of your direct working hours.
- Location Freedom: Digital products can be created and accessed from anywhere in the world with Wi-Fi connection. This global

reach allows you to connect with a vast audience without geographical constraints.

- Financial Freedom: With digital products, there are virtually no limits to the number of sales you can make. Unlike physical products, digital courses and trainings don't require restocking, and there's no cap on the number of students you can serve.

Digital products in education, such as online courses and training programs, offer a unique blend of scalability and accessibility. They allow you to package your knowledge and expertise into a format that can be repeatedly sold without additional production costs. This model not only maximizes profit margins but also extends the reach of your impactful content.

Here is how the law of domination works when it comes to a digital product.

- You produce a solution to a problem in the form of a mini-course, perhaps you turn your

mini workshop into a digital product #BeFruitful
- Since it's digital, it already has the ability to be replicated, built right into it #Multiply
- Now it's time to get it in the hands of others, without your direct daily input, to do this we create a sales funnel, this is #Replenish
- Finally give your intellectual property a name so that you can standout and begin to subdue the marketplace #Subdue

Let's Review…

This is a perfect example of how to apply the law of domination in business. The business of digital products is creating a shift in how we approach business and education. They offer a great opportunity to achieve time, location, and financial freedom, all while breaking free from the constraints of traditional business models.

Can you imagine the financial potential that digital products offer?

Good, now let's get to the money! See the money math example:

A. Fitzgerald Hardnett

THE MONEY MATH FOR DIGITAL PRODUCTS

Create a digital product that you sell for
$297, sell just 34 a month
$297 x 34 = $10,098 /month

If you do that for 12 months
$10,098 x 12 = $121,176 /year

this is equivalent to you working
40 hrs a week x 50 weeks = 2000 hrs
getting paid $60.59/hr

Even if you only sold 10 a month:
10 x $297 = $2970

$2970 x 12 months = $35,640
which is a F/T job paying $17.82/hr

This is the power of digital products, now imagine you had 5 products like this working for you 24/7/365 days a year! Would this allow you the time & financial freedom you desire?

Now you can see why I strongly suggest that *EVERY* Christian should start a digital education business using their existing knowledge and skills?

You might be wondering, "Alright Fitz, I understand the opportunity, but how do I begin? And, how do I decide which skill to use, or what problem to solve using one of these three methods?"

In the following section, I'll address these questions. I'll guide you on how to identify a profitable problem that matches your skills and expertise. This is thoroughly explained in the chapter titled "Absolute Clarity."

ABSOLUTE CLARITY

My actual gift in the Body of Christ is that of a teacher, I've had the unique opportunity to hone this gift over the last 21 years. This path has been shaped by diverse experiences, each adding depth and understanding to my ability to simplify complex concepts.

Along this journey, I've had the privilege of nurturing minds and guiding understanding of children (as a parent, uncle and teacher in the Alexandria City Public School System) as well as adults (as a business consultant and motivational speaker). I embraced each of these opportunities to refine my approach and make learning accessible and engaging for all.

God has given me a 6ix step framework that is the foundation for every idea, product or opportunity that we encounter. I take all my clients through this framework because it is so powerful. I call this framework Absolute Clarity™ and the acronym that I use is POP & MOM and I want to share it with you as well.

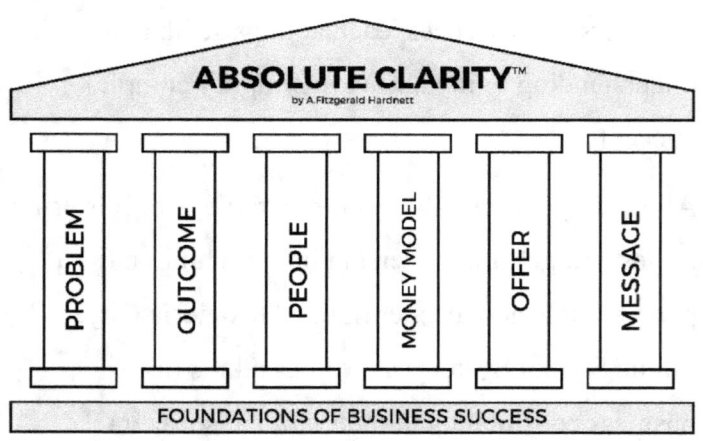

Here is an overview of the Absolute Clarity™ process:

Problem: What problem does this solve?

Outcome: What is the outcome? What can they do now that wasn't possible before?

People: Who wants this outcome, because they have this problem?

Money Model: How are you going to monetize your solution? How much should it be?

Offer: What are you actually selling to people? Note that it must be juicy and irresistible!

Message: What should you say to the people to get their attention and pull them in to consider your offer to help?

Being able to clearly answer these six questions will set you up to dominate your marketplace.

Let's look at each one of the 6ix in more detail...

What's In Your Hand?

PROBLEM OUTCOME PEOPLE

P: The Problem You Solve

This step is all about clarity. What problem do you solve? Note that it doesn't have to be a business-related issue. It could be anything people need help with and are willing to pay for. Whether it's teaching double-dutch, baking a cake, or making money online – what's *your* area of expertise?

What's that painfully profitable problem you can address? Think about what people often ask you to help them with. – this is a clue as to what problem people trust you to solve for them.

What painful problem can you solve for people? Over the years you have amassed a certain set of **S**kills, **T**alents, **A**bilities and **R**esourcefulness, and when you put it together, it makes you a STAR!

See… I know your next question, because it was my dilemma too. You say Fitz, I can do a lot of things well, how do I choose? I know that you can do a lot of things well, that comes as no surprise, because you were made in the image and likeness of GOD, remember? You are a creative speaking spirit with the power to dominate.

I have three main requirements that I present to my students to consider when they are trying to figure out what problem to solve. Here they are…

You must have the skills to solve the problem, you can't fumble your way through this. People are looking for answers and investing their money, they have a right to competent solutions.

1. Experience is important. Please do not offer something that you just learned, or are learning. Choose something that you have proven results with. It will be better for all involved.
2. Excitement! Pick a problem that energizes you, something that you will enjoy doing over and over again without despising it. From my experience, it's a lot easier to do a good job on projects that you enjoy doing. Remember, this is your business, you build it how YOU

want. I encourage you to add enjoyment to the mix.

3. The last point is not included in the diagram, but I mention it, because it is critical to your success. Make sure that there is a big enough market to sustain your digital business.

S.E.E. Method

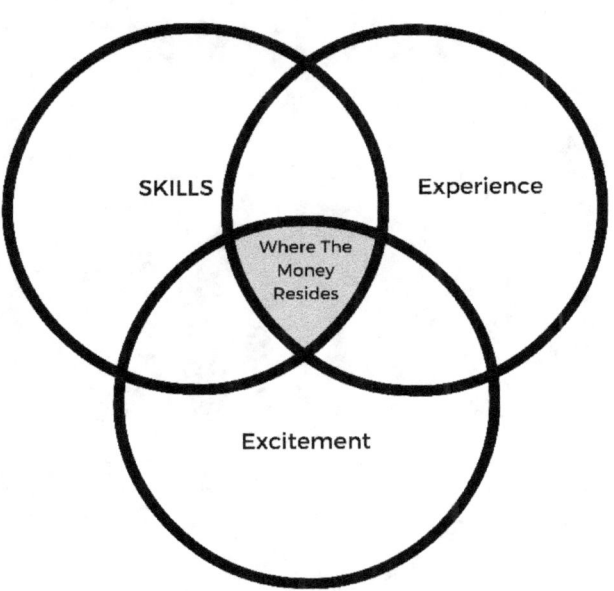

What's In Your Hand?

PROBLEM **OUTCOME** PEOPLE

O: The Outcome

Once you've identified the problem, what is the outcome or the transformation that solving that problem provides for them? What are they now able to DO? What is their **D**esired **O**utcome?

When people come to you, it's because they have a problem and they believe you can help them transform their world. I teach my clients and students that they become a transportation company, no different than an airline like Delta, or a train like Amtrak. This is the best way that I've found to teach this important concept.

Fitz Fact™

When you offer someone your solution, you are literally changing their location, from pain to paradise. From not being able to do something, to now, having it done!

Here are three powerful questions that you need to be able to answer that will help you clearly define and communicate the outcome of your product or services:

1. Where are they? This ties directly into the P, in POP. What problem do they have? What pain are they in? In the transportation analogy it's where are they starting from?
2. Where are they going? What is their new destination or desired outcome? Where do they want to be after hiring you for help? The transportation analogy… where are they traveling to?
3. How fast do they want to get there? This will help determine what you offer them. For instance, if we use our three ways to make money online using what we already know, have, and do, as an example, each of them can solve their problem, just at different speeds. If we were to rank our transportation options it would look like this:
    a. Moderate - Digital products a 'Do It Yourself' solution, which is faster than them trying to figure it out on

their own because you have given them the blueprint.

b. Faster - Mini Workshop: a 'Done With You' solution.

c. Fastest - Consulting is, "Here's exactly what to do, and, if you'd like, it can be Done For You."

Each of these solutions will take the people you are called to serve to their desired destination. It's just a matter of choice, how fast they want to get there, and how fast can you take them?

I have a process that I teach that will give you a clear visual of this whole process, I call it "The Path To Paradise."

What's In Your Hand?

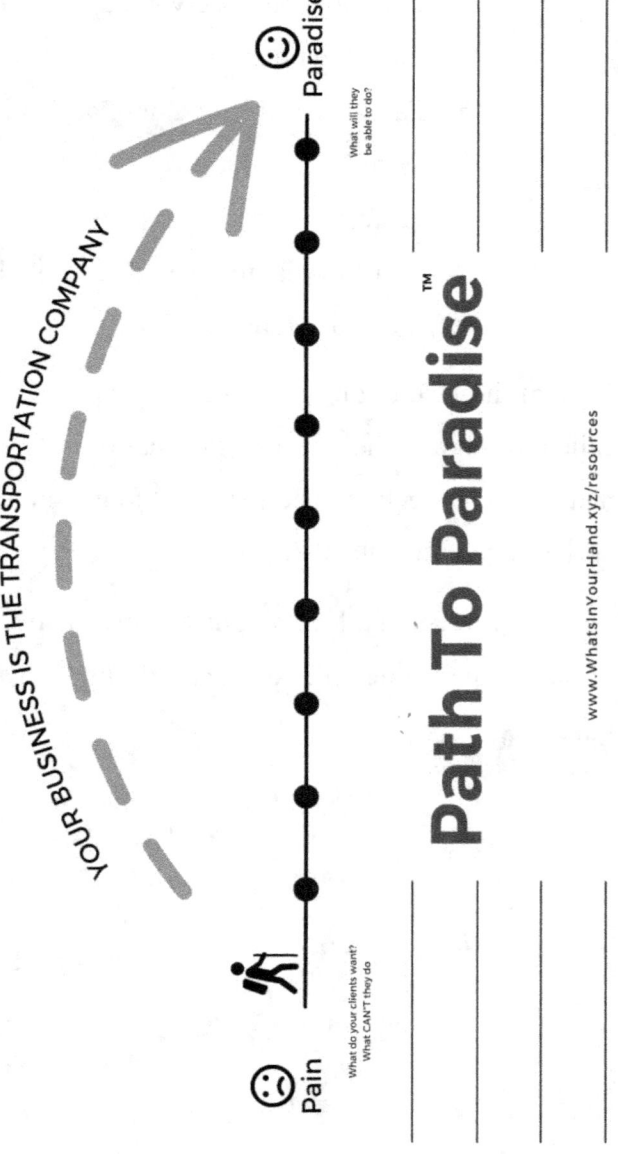

Here's how it works: On the left under the word pain, you list all the problems that your client has, the things that they can't currently do, and where they are starting from, these must be problems that you can "S.E.E." (refer to how to pick a problem SEE method)

The dots on the path correspond to each problem. Your solution must address each of their concerns in the order that they are likely to face them.

Once each problem is addressed, they will now be in paradise, their desired location.

On the right under the word paradise, you would list all the things that they can now do. Having this level of clarity protects you, by providing a well-defined destination and contractual end to your engagement with them.

This also helps to build your business with continuity, and here's why. Every solution should cause another problem that you have the skills to solve.

This means if they need to spend more money, it shouldn't be a problem. You already fixed their first problem, so now they believe in you and trust you even more.

PROBLEM OUTCOME **PEOPLE**

P: The People

Who wants this outcome? These are the people who face the problem you solve. Understanding your audience is crucial – they are the ones who find your solution valuable enough to pay for. Think about what makes someone an ideal client for you.

- Who would benefit most from what you offer?
- What makes them a dream client?
- What makes them less than ideal?

Think about your process, and what is needed for it to be a breeze for you to get that client results? If you could ONLY get paid after they got the promised result, what would these people have to have, and what must they believe? When you take this approach, you will absolutely identify your dream clients.

What's In Your Hand?

MONEY MODEL OFFER MESSAGING

M: Money Model

This section is all about choosing your monetization model, setting revenue goals and then reverse engineering your numbers with an actual plan to hit them. It provides the proper context of the amount of effort it's going to take to achieve your vision. People lie, numbers don't. Trust the numbers.

There are a series of questions that you must answer and calculate for this information to be helpful to you.

1. What is your annual top line revenue goal (TLRG)? Your annual TLRG is how much money you want to generate in the next 12 months.
2. Which of these three business models are you going to use to get there? Or do you have the capacity to implement a combination of these opportunities?

    a. If it's a combination what percentage of that top line revenue goal TLRG will each part comprise?

For example, if you say your TLRG is $120,000 and you are going to use two of the methods, consulting is going to be 75% and workshops are going to be 25%.

(insert year) Revenue Goal $120,000

Consulting 75% = $120,000 x .75 = $90,000

Workshops 25%= $120,000 x .25 = $30,000

Next, you must choose what to charge for your solution, because this will tell you how many that you need to sell to hit your revenue goals.

For example, Let's say you've decided that you're charging $3K for consulting and $100 for the workshop

Consulting $90,000 ÷ $3000 = 30 clients needed

Workshops $30,000 ÷ $100 =300 students needed

These are the raw numbers, next you need to answer these questions:

How many leads do I need to talk to before I get a sale that turns into a client or student?

To answer this question, do these steps:

- Look at your history. If you get in front of 100 QUALIFIED leads, how many sales will you make? If you can close 10 out of 100 then your ratio is 10:100 and your closing percentage is 10%, if 5:100 then it's 5%.
- If you don't have any history to go off of, assume that you will convert one out of 100 which is a 1:100 ratio, so that's a 1%.
- So to figure out how many sales conversations you need to have with qualified leads take (the # of sales needed ÷ by your closing percentage).

$30 \div 10\% = 300$ qualified lead conversations

$30 \div 5\% = 600$ qualified lead conversations

$30 \div 1\% = 3000$ qualified lead conversations

- How many prospects do I need to get in front of, in order to get a qualified lead?
- (the number of qualified lead conversations ÷ by your closing percentage)
- What kind of lead magnet do I need to create that my dream clients would find valuable enough to exchange their contact information so that I can build a list of qualified leads?
- How much visibility do I need in order to reach enough suspects that will turn into prospects?

This money model gets deep, this is why I loved when Elisha told the widow woman to borrow not a few, because her breakthrough, just like yours will require you to go beyond what you think is reasonable.

Doing this part is challenging I know, but we do challenging things every day and this is so necessary for your success. Let's get to it…

Bonus Content

Go to www.WhatsInYourHand.xyz/resources

for access to a video of me breaking this Money Model down. You will also find checklists and other cool stuff that I made to make this process easier to understand

What's In Your Hand?

MONEY MODEL **OFFER** MESSAGING

O: Offer

The offer is what you actually are doing, or including, in your product or service. It is made up of individual components that when joined together produce the overall promise that you make in your messaging.

Each thing that you include should be a valuable and necessary step to their desired destination. Any bonuses that you add should aid in the delivery of the outcome faster, or it should address the next step in their journey.

At the end of the day, your offer should be so irresistibly juicy, that folks can't pass it up. When they examine it, they say to themselves, I get all of this for only $xx,xxx?

Authors Note

Don't make the mistake of just jamming your offers full of stuff. That is NOT how you make them more valuable and desirable. In fact, I encourage you to have less stuff. Offer only what is necessary for them to achieve their desired outcome. #LessIsMore

Fitz Fact™

"Your offer is the actions you take to deliver results, but what you're really selling is the confidence that you understand their problems and have a system to help them get the results they want."

MONEY MODEL OFFER **MESSAGING**

M: Messaging

Messaging is the cornerstone of your business's communication strategy, it's the ultimate bait, the magnetic force that attracts your audience. It is the sixth and final, yet crucial, piece of your marketing foundation.

Your message is how you speak to the world and how you draw in the right people. Like the Bible says in John 10:27, "My sheep know my voice, and they won't follow a stranger's voice." Your audience will know and follow your special voice, even with all the other noise around. Your message is crucial; it must be clear and powerful to unmistakably attract the exact people you want to work with.

Fitz Fact™

"Your message is your first lead magnet, and it determines the quality of your clients"

To effectively call out your audience, you must be crystal clear about the **P**roblem you're solving, the **O**utcome you're delivering, and the **P**eople you're called to help. The more clarity and confidence you have around these three elements, the stronger and more potent your messaging will be. These pillars are even more important than what your business does or the specifics of what you're selling.

Without this level of clarity and confidence woven into the very fabric of your message, your audience will remain disengaged and unresponsive.

"Effective messaging is always about the people, you're here to serve, it's not about you."

The content that you create should make your ideal client feel seen and understood. This connection is what makes your message resonate.

Knowing your audience is critical.

Vague messaging attracts the wrong people, which leads to frustration on both sides. Your message should reflect your audience's needs, beliefs, aspirations and patterns.

Recall our earlier discussion about being created in the image and likeness of God; a creative problem solver, who uses words to shape their world. Messaging is the catalyst for this power.

Fitz Fact™

The words you use in your outbound marketing materials create the reality you live in. They attract the clients you want or don't want!

Remember, effective messaging is about creating a world where your ideal clients feel understood and seen by your content. A world where you stand out as the obvious choice to do business with!

What's In Your Hand?

UNIT 3:
CALL TO ACTION

What's In Your Hand?

GRATITUDE & SUPPORT

2 Corinthians 4:15

All this is for your benefit, so that the grace that is reaching more and more people may cause thanksgiving to overflow to the glory of God.

To My Incredible Supporters & Readers,

As I pen these words, my heart is brimming with gratitude and warmth for each one of you. This book, a labor of love and dedication, would not have been possible without your unwavering faith and financial support.

From the very beginning, even before a single word of this book was written, you believed in me. Your belief wasn't just in the idea of this book, but in me as a business person with a message to share. This kind of trust is rare and precious, and I am deeply humbled and honored by it.

I am aware that this journey took longer than anticipated, and your patience and understanding through this extended process have been nothing short of remarkable. It's not just the wait; it's the encouragement, the gentle inquiries, and the unwavering belief that kept me going through the challenging times of this journey.

You didn't just sponsor a book; you sponsored a dream, my dream. You helped create a piece of art, and a slice of human thought and emotion geared to create impact in the world.

As you flip through these pages, I hope you just don't see my words, but the reflection of *your* belief and support. This book is as much yours as it is mine. It is a testament to what can be achieved when people come together in support of a shared vision.

Thank you for being a part of this incredible journey. I am eternally grateful to each one of you.

With Heartfelt Gratitude,

Fitz

What's In Your Hand?

THANK YOU, CHAMPIONS OF CHANGE,

Leading with heart and generosity at lightning speed!

"My Love, I am so excited to see what God is going to do through this book. God has given you so much wisdom, talent and passion and I am glad to see you share it with the world! The world needs your light! Let's Go….Boom Baby!" - **Asha J. Hardnett**

"May you continue to allow Lord God Jehovah to lead and guide you. Never "settle". -Love and hugs Mom -**Fredicia Raines Hardnett**

"Fitz, I'm so proud of you, now the world gets to truly see your genius" - **Dr. Desirae King**

"Wishing you all of the success and a wonderful launch" - **De'Geon "Money" Briggs**

"You are the GOAT at marketing! EVERY SINGLE time I did what you said, we made a boatload of money" - **Lisa Dunnigan**

"We help you take your business idea and turn it into income!" **-D.L. Hatchett & Associates**

"I am so proud to have you as my dad, words can't explain how grateful and important you have been to my life. You have shown me what a real man and Hardnett is supposed to be. I have no idea what I would have done without you!"

-Maximilian J. Hardnett

GRATEFUL FOR MY SUPPORTERS,
The Dynamic Force Behind This Journey Stepping Up with Passion and Support!

"Congrats on your book Fitzgerald & thank you for all you do!"- Angel Conway, Self Care Coach At Because I Care 2, we Equip & Encourage moms to take care of herself. Book a Consult today. https://payhip.com/b/sevTV .

"Your guidance and support inspire us to reach new heights. Thank you for being an incredible mentor."

Love, Miami Car Cartel, John and Gloria Baranski

"You are Unique, Divine and Magical"
- from your Afro Unicorn friends

"Fitz is worthy of so much, and I am so excited to have had the opportunity to be included in this achievement!" -Angeliese Wisdom

Bookkeeping with Wisdom LLC

Generate a 6-Figure Recurring Revenue In 6 Months or Less With a Revolutionary New Done-For-You Business Model: - Greg Russell

https://ConsistentCashflowMachine.com/

"Bravo, Fitz! "What's In Your Hands' is a testament to your expertise. Proud to support you". DorothyVB Helping you automate your lead follow-up,
-AKB Small Business Marketing

Congrats SUPERSTAR! Keep shining and using your God-given gifts to help us on our journey to be successful entrepreneurs. May everything you touch be blessed and multiplied. -Trice Smith, UnBossed Apparel

Witnessing your growth has been a privilege. Here's to your continued success! -Tim Bing

Additional Early Supporters

Makeda Rodriguez

Anthony MrGuru Feaster MET

It Takes a Village Childcare

T.N.S FASHION CUT

Coach Tee- The Tee Academy

Shamara 'Star' Cox

Jenny Benzie

Clean Concepts Mobile Det LLC

Dwight Francis

Sharon Sills

Again, thank you all

-Fitz

ARISE & SHINE... YOUR TIME HAS COME

As we conclude this journey, I hope you're brimming with excitement about the possibilities within your reach.

Isaiah 60:1 hits home with a powerful call to action: "Arise, shine; for your light has come!"

This is not just a wake-up call—it's a command to elevate ourselves, to stand up in the fullness of our potential because God's glory is upon us.

We are living in a time when darkness engulfs the world, but that same darkness is our cue to shine even brighter.

Think about it this way—have you ever been to your local hardware store or nursery, like Home Depot or Lowe's? They have a lawn & garden section that contains shelves full of seed packets, each with a picture on the front showing what the seeds inside have the potential to become.

But here's the catch: if those seeds stay sealed up in their packets, sitting on a shelf, they'll never grow. They're in the wrong environment.

Just like those seeds, many of us are not in the right place to flourish.

We've got this picture of what we could be, but we're stuck in a space that doesn't challenge or nurture us, scriptures say "iron sharpens iron" until we are in a space that challenges us, we won't realize our full potential.

All breakthroughs started by taking inventory of what a person has and then using that to change the world.

Both Moses and David reached their full potential and changed the world by setting people free. These stories are a powerful reminder that the giants in your life can be conquered by simply using what's in your hands.

So…What's in Your Hand?

Now you have two choices, get inspired and put this book on your shelf, check off an imaginary box of completion but take no further action, that's what the average Believer would do.

But I believe that you are above average, that's why you finished this book to start the process of transformation. You know you have skills and you just needed to know WHAT to do. This book covers that and provides some of the how, but if you want help customizing these solutions to fit you and your gifts, I invite you to consider joining one of my programs to get more personalized help. The principles and strategies we've explored are more than just concepts; they are actual winning plays currently being run in the marketplace, and they are waiting to be used by you!

If you're ready to elevate your business using the insights from this book, we've got just the thing for you.

THE OFFER CALL™

In line with this philosophy, I've developed two programs designed to empower you along your journey. These solutions are 'Slingshot' and '$10K Play.'

Slingshot:

This program is a nod to the very tool David used to slay Goliath. 'Slingshot' is about gaining marketing momentum through having absolute clarity around your core. It walks you through the 6ix foundational pillars outlined in this book – M.O.M. & P.O.P.

At the conclusion of the Slingshot program, you will gain unmatched clarity and confidence, essential for distinguishing yourself as the dominant force in the market you were meant to be.

With this newfound insight, you will be confidently equipped to answer the following four critical questions…

1. What specific problem do you solve?
2. Who do you serve, and what makes them the ideal fit for you?
3. What should you sell, and at what price point?
4. What messaging will effectively attract your dream clients?

Having total mastery of these are the cornerstone of your success, ensuring you're not just participating in the market but leading it with certainty and vision.

The 10K Play:

If you know that you want to launch a digital product/ education business, "The 10K Play" is designed specifically for you. This intimate, high-touch group coaching program is tailored for purpose-driven entrepreneurs who are eager to create and launch their first digital mini-course.

In "The 10K Play," you'll learn how to develop a digital product that not only has the potential to generate over $10,000 a month but also provides you with the means to support your goals and make a significant impact for the Kingdom in the world.

The core focus of this program is to guide you through the process of creating a compelling digital course and achieving your initial sales milestone of $1,000 all the way to $10k and beyond. We provide you with all the essential tools and personalized support needed to turn your ideas into income.

For more details and to join us on this transformative journey, visit www.10kPlay.com.

I am genuinely delighted that you've been part of this journey. The insights and strategies in this book are just the beginning. With 'Slingshot' and 'The 10K Play', you have the opportunity to apply what you've learned and take concrete steps towards your goals. Remember, the power lies in what's in your hand – it's time to use it to shape your future.

Speak To Us

Need something specific, reach out to us, head over to www.talktofitz.com/book.

There, you'll encounter a brief questionnaire about your business or your budding business idea. It's our way of getting to know you before our conversation.

Fill in the details, and voilà – you'll be directed to a calendar with a list of available dates and times. Pick the one that works best for you. Add this date to your calendar.

After booking, you'll be greeted by a confirmation page. This isn't just any page; it's your gateway to getting the most out of our call. It includes essential instructions and a video that demystifies what working with us looks like. Plus, you'll find testimonials and case studies of my clients, giving you a head start in understanding our approach.

During our call, we'll dive deep into your business, pinpointing challenges and exploring potential solutions. If we find that we're a match, we'll guide you through our collaboration process. You'll have the freedom to decide if joining our client roster is the right move for you.

There's absolutely no pressure.

Regardless, this call promises to be an eye-opener, offering you valuable insights.

So, don't delay – visit www.talktofitz.com/book and schedule your call today.

Let's go on this journey to business growth together!

ABOUT
A. FITZGERALD HARDNETT

A.Fitzgerald Hardnett is America's Favorite Faith-Based Digital Marketing Strategist. He is known as The Visibility Genius™, because he helps entrepreneurs make money online FASTER by increasing their visibility using social media advertising and video marketing.

He's the Founder & CEO of Social Leverage, an entrepreneurial education & consulting company with brand extensions in e-commerce. His motto is…

"If people never pay you any attention, they'll never pay you any money!!"

A. Fitzgerald Hardnett

RESOURCES

Unit 1

Believer's Business Building Blocks…………....pg16
How to Choose Life graphic………………......pg21
The Law of Domination ………………….…..pg43

Unit 2

Money Math for Digital Products………….... pg.73
Absolute Clarity™ Framework……………... pg.76
S.E.E. Method ……………………....…..……. pg.81
Path to Paradise ……………………………....... pg.86

Resources found at:
www.WhatsInYourHand.xyz/resources

15 Word based affirmation…………...…….. Download
Getting Started Tools …………………… Download
How To Create A Quick Win Workshop....Download
Bonus Content: Money Model……….…….… Video
Bonus Content: Money Model ……………Checklist
Discovery Call: wwww.TalkToFitz.com

REFLECTION QUESTIONS

These reflective questions are designed for book clubs, groups, organizations and individuals who are looking to truly maximize the information within this book.

Revenue Revolution

- What is your motivation to discover how to make money online using what you already know, have, and do?
- Why now?
- If you don't figure this out, who loses? Whose life will be impacted most, if you don't get this right? List their names.
- This is important because if your why doesn't make you cry, then you'll quit, there will be/are hundreds of reasons for you to quit, but you only need 1 reason to continue, Identify those reasons here!!
- What are 3 things that you are good at? What is that thing that you can do exceptionally

well, but you see others getting paid handsomely to do?

- Are you willing to commit to only provide solutions to problems that the marketplace is paying big money to have solved, meaning you will only solve in-demand problems?
- Are you willing to serve the marketplace by SELLING your solution for a handsome profit?
- Are you open to executing a proven plan that will put you on the path to profits? If so go here and schedule a call with myself or one of my teammates www.WorkWithFitz.com

NOTES

What's In Your Hand?

A. Fitzgerald Hardnett

www.ingramcontent.com/pod-product-compliance
Lightning Source LLC
Chambersburg PA
CBHW071405290426
44108CB00014B/1690